10/12

PHEASANT HUNTING

BY BLAKE POUND

BELLWETHER MEDIA • MINNEAPOLIS, MN

Jump into the cockpit and take flight with Pilot books. Your journey will take you on high-energy adventures as you learn about all that is wild, weird, fascinating, and fun!

This edition first published in 2013 by Bellwether Media, Inc.

No part of this publication may be reproduced in whole or in part without written permission of the publisher. For information regarding permission, write to Bellwether Media, Inc., Attention: Permissions Department, 5357 Penn Avenue South, Minneapolis, MN 55419.

Library of Congress Cataloging-in-Publication Data

Pound, Blake.
Pheasant hunting / by Blake Pound.
    p. cm. – (Pilot books: outdoor adventures)
Includes bibliographical references and index.
Summary: "Engaging images accompany information about pheasant hunting. The combination of high-interest subject matter and narrative text is intended for students in grades 3 through 7"–Provided by publisher.
ISBN 978-1-60014-801-9 (hardcover : alk. paper)
1. Pheasant shooting–Juvenile literature. I. Title.
SK325.P5P68 2013
799.2'46252–dc23   2012007879

Printed in the United States of America, North Mankato, MN.

TABLE OF CONTENTS

OPEN SEASON

A hunter makes his way across an open prairie. His trained bird dog walks quietly at his side. The pair moves into the wind toward a nest of pheasants. The alert pheasants hear the hunter's footsteps. They break and run in the other direction, but a small pond blocks their path. Unable to swim, the birds flap their wings and take flight.

The dog stops suddenly and points his body toward the flock. The hunter raises his shotgun and aims at a rooster. He fires as the birds cross the sky. The rooster falls to the ground. The dog rushes to retrieve the bird while the hunter reloads his weapon. Pheasant season has begun!

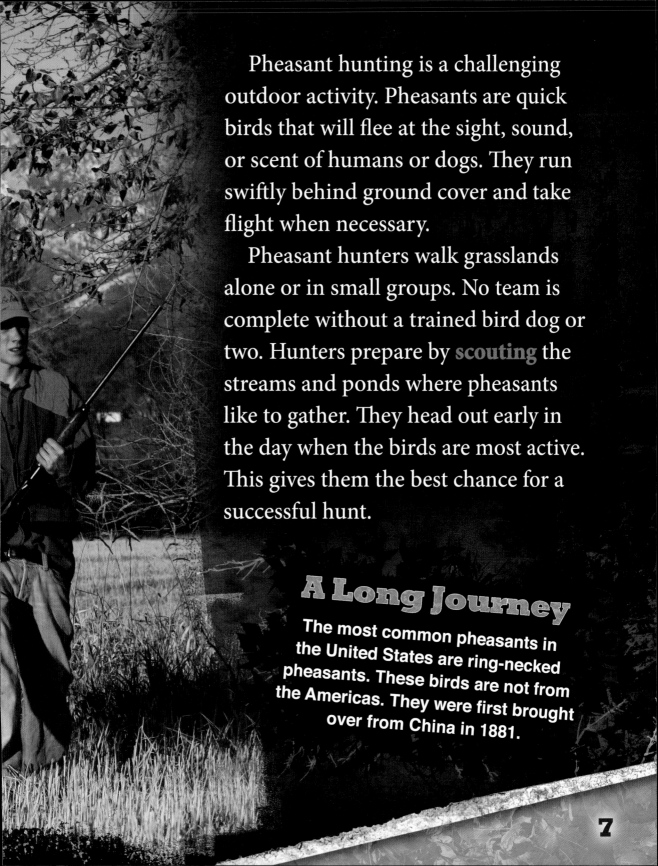

Pheasant hunting is a challenging outdoor activity. Pheasants are quick birds that will flee at the sight, sound, or scent of humans or dogs. They run swiftly behind ground cover and take flight when necessary.

Pheasant hunters walk grasslands alone or in small groups. No team is complete without a trained bird dog or two. Hunters prepare by scouting the streams and ponds where pheasants like to gather. They head out early in the day when the birds are most active. This gives them the best chance for a successful hunt.

A Long Journey

The most common pheasants in the United States are ring-necked pheasants. These birds are not from the Americas. They were first brought over from China in 1881.

DOGS, GUNS, AND SAFETY

Pheasant hunters and their dogs walk miles over quiet hills and fields in search of their prey. Dogs lead hunters to pheasants and **flush** them from the tall grass. Then they retrieve the birds that have been shot down. If a bird is only wounded, a dog kills it before bringing it back to the hunter. Some dogs are natural pointers. Others have sharp **instincts** for retrieving or flushing.

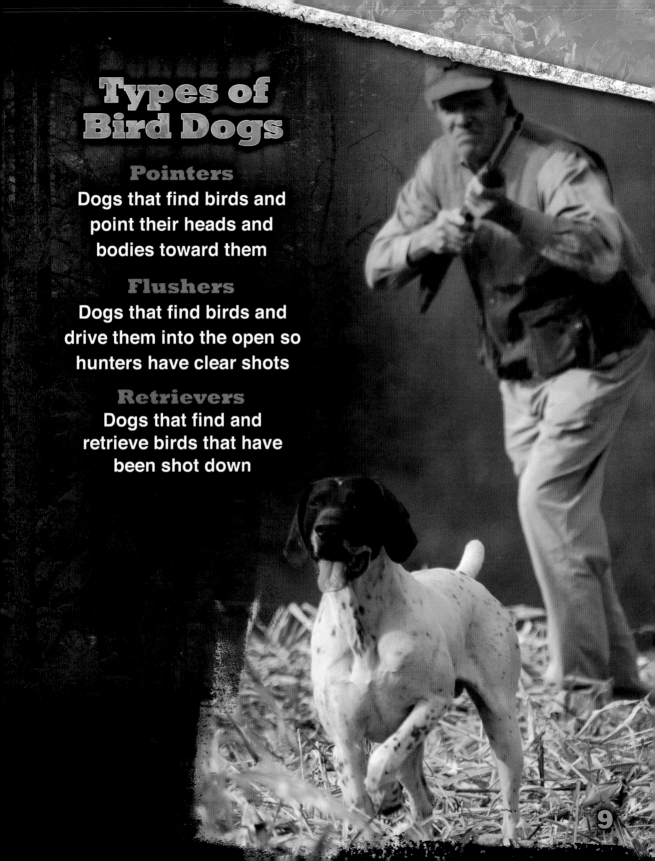

Types of Bird Dogs

Pointers
Dogs that find birds and point their heads and bodies toward them

Flushers
Dogs that find birds and drive them into the open so hunters have clear shots

Retrievers
Dogs that find and retrieve birds that have been shot down

9

Hunters spend a lot of time training their bird dogs. They teach their dogs to respond to whistles, hand signals, and quiet voice commands. They also expose their dogs to the sound of gunshots so the dogs are not frightened on the hunt.

Untrained dogs can ruin a hunt. Dogs that run too far ahead of a group can scare away pheasants before the hunters are in range. Dogs that chase after other animals give pheasants more time to escape. If a dog is not properly trained in retrieving, it may damage a pheasant.

Pheasant hunters use shotguns to **bag** their birds. Shotguns scatter small pellets called shot over a wide area. This makes it easier for pheasant hunters to hit targets in the air. Hunters choose a shotgun **gauge** that best suits them. Lower-gauge shotguns hold larger **cartridges**. Larger cartridges give hunters more **recoil**.

cartridge

Types of Shotguns

Pump-action
Loads a cartridge when the
hunter pumps the gun

Semi-automatic
Fires a single cartridge every
time the trigger is pulled

Double-barreled
Fires cartridges from two
barrels, one after the other

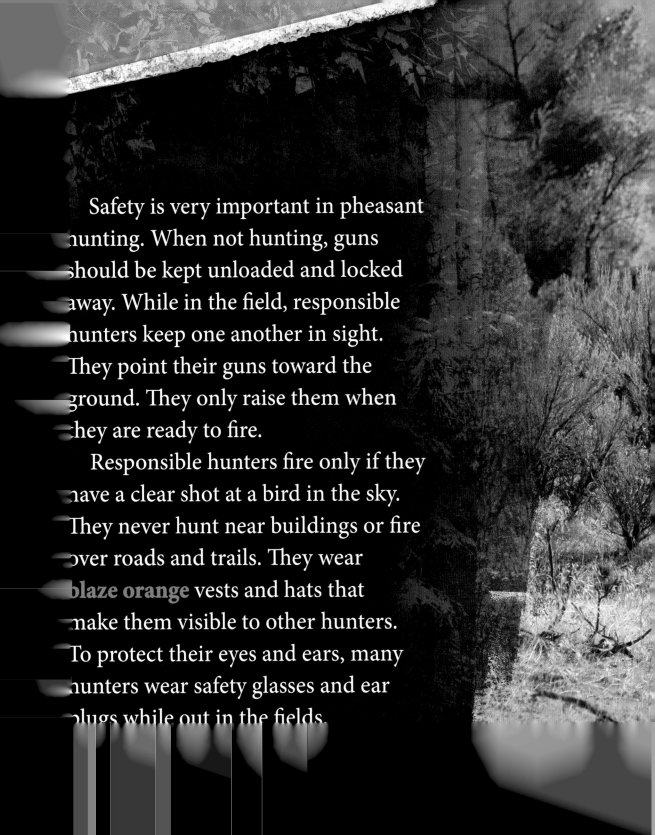

Safety is very important in pheasant hunting. When not hunting, guns should be kept unloaded and locked away. While in the field, responsible hunters keep one another in sight. They point their guns toward the ground. They only raise them when they are ready to fire.

Responsible hunters fire only if they have a clear shot at a bird in the sky. They never hunt near buildings or fire over roads and trails. They wear **blaze orange** vests and hats that make them visible to other hunters. To protect their eyes and ears, many hunters wear safety glasses and ear plugs while out in the fields.

PLANNING AND RESPECT

Hunters need to plan before they head out to the fields. Every state requires hunters to purchase a hunting **license**. Each state has its own hunting season and limits the number of pheasants a hunter can shoot and keep. Most states do not allow hunters to shoot **hens**. This helps keep pheasant populations strong.

Hunters should scout the land where they are going to hunt. Studying maps and exploring the area are great ways to find pheasant hiding spots. Hunters often seek out areas with thick brush and weeds. They know that pheasants take shelter in this heavy ground cover.

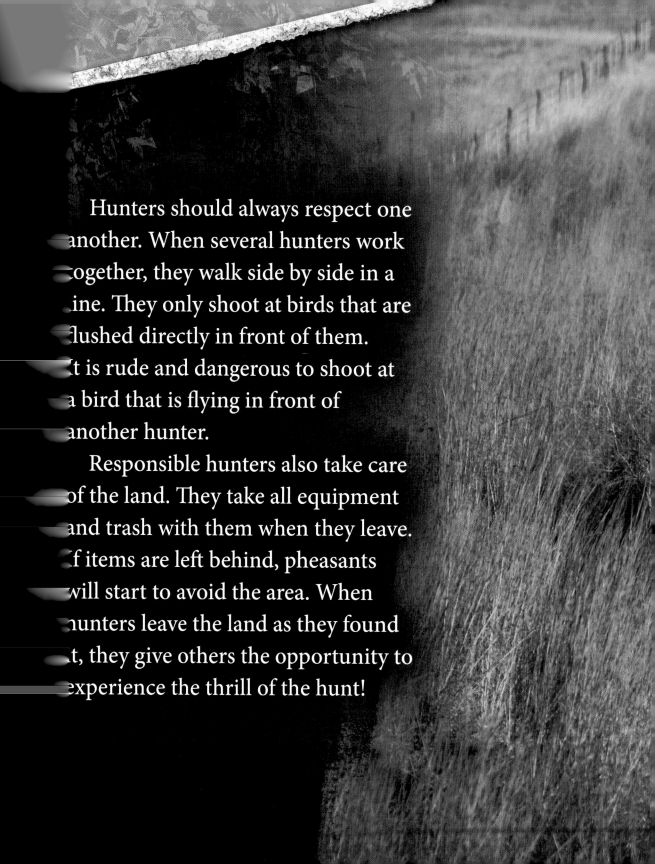

Hunters should always respect one another. When several hunters work together, they walk side by side in a line. They only shoot at birds that are flushed directly in front of them. It is rude and dangerous to shoot at a bird that is flying in front of another hunter.

Responsible hunters also take care of the land. They take all equipment and trash with them when they leave. If items are left behind, pheasants will start to avoid the area. When hunters leave the land as they found it, they give others the opportunity to experience the thrill of the hunt!

Helping Hands

Many hunters join conservation groups. These organizations work to protect and expand pheasant habitats.

SOUTH DAKOTA: PHEASANT COUNTRY

The grass prairies that cover South Dakota make the state one of the best places for pheasant hunting. Hunters and their dogs often stay at lodges that own the surrounding land. Some lodges build their own pheasant habitats with grasses and crops that attract the birds.

Most pheasant hunting lodges provide **guides** with trained bird dogs to take hunters into the fields. Hunters track birds through cornfields and across grassy hills. They stay alert to their surroundings and anticipate the sound of rustling feathers. At any moment, a rooster may take to the air and offer the chance to bag a big South Dakota pheasant!

A Big Haul

In 2010, hunters shot more than 1.8 million pheasants in South Dakota.

GLOSSARY

bag—to shoot down and capture

bird dog—a dog trained to help hunters track, flush, and retrieve birds

blaze orange—the color most hunters are required to wear for safety

cartridges—shells that contain everything needed to fire shot from a shotgun

flush—to chase out into the open from a place of hiding

gauge—a measurement related to the size of a shotgun barrel

guides—professionals who help hunters plan hunting trips and often lead them into fields

hens—female pheasants

instincts—natural ways of behaving

license—a document that gives legal permission to do an activity

recoil—the kickback of a gun upon firing

rooster—a male pheasant

scouting—exploring an area to learn more about it

TO LEARN MORE

At the Library

MacRae, Sloan. *Upland Hunting: Pheasant, Quail, and Other Game Birds.* New York, N.Y.: PowerKids Press, 2011.

Martin, Michael. *Pheasant Hunting.* Mankato, Minn.: Capstone Press, 2008.

Mebane, Jeanie. *Pheasant Hunting.* Mankato, Minn.: Capstone Press, 2012.

On the Web

Learning more about pheasant hunting is as easy as 1, 2, 3.

1. Go to www.factsurfer.com.

2. Enter "pheasant hunting" into the search box.

3. Click the "Surf" button and you will see a list of related Web sites.

With factsurfer.com, finding more information is just a click away.

INDEX